D1402858

Matt Groening and The Simpsons

Other titles in the *Contemporary Cartoon Creators* series include:

Seth MacFarlane and Family Guy

Stephen Hillenburg and SpongeBob SquarePants

Trey Parker, Matt Stone, and South Park

Matt Groening and The Simpsons

Stuart A. Kallen

San Diego, CA

About the Author

Stuart A. Kallen is the author of more than three hundred nonfiction books for children and young adults. He has written on topics ranging from the theory of relativity to the history of rock and roll. In addition, Kallen has written award-winning children's videos and television scripts. In his spare time, he is a singer/songwriter/guitarist in San Diego.

© 2016 ReferencePoint Press, Inc.
Printed in the United States

For more information, contact:
ReferencePoint Press, Inc.
PO Box 27779
San Diego, CA 92198
www. ReferencePointPress.com

ALL RIGHTS RESERVED.
No part of this work covered by the copyright hereon may be reproduced or used in any form or by any means—graphic, electronic, or mechanical, including photocopying, recording, taping, web distribution, or information storage retrieval systems—without the written permission of the publisher.

LIBRARY OF CONGRESS CATALOGING-IN-PUBLICATION DATA

Kallen, Stuart A., 1955-
Matt Groening and The Simpsons / by Stuart A. Kallen.
    pages cm. -- (Contemporary cartoon creators series)
Includes bibliographical references and index.
ISBN-13: 978-1-60152-784-4 (hardback)
ISBN-10: 1-60152-784-5 (hardback)
1. Groening, Matt--Juvenile literature. 2. Cartoonists--United States--Biography--Juvenile literature. I. Title.
PN6727.G755Z65 2015
741.5'092--dc23
[B]
                                                                    2014035198

CONTENTS

For the Love of "Everyman"

The term *satire* can be traced back to ancient Rome in the first century BCE, when the writer Horace used lighthearted humor and playful exaggeration to gently mock and criticize human folly. In modern times satire has been used to address social evils. Writers wield wit as a weapon to expose society's shortcomings and use parody to spoof self-serving politicians and celebrities.

Matt Groening, cocreator and executive producer of the animated television shows *The Simpsons* and *Futurama*, fits the definition of a satirist. His talents for mocking, criticizing, and exposing the foolishness of modern culture have brought him exceptional success. *The Simpsons* is the longest-running show in television history. *Futurama*, while less successful, has also received widespread critical acclaim.

Love of the "Everyman"

Both of Groening's shows have earned numerous awards and generated billions in sales of T-shirts, comic books, toys, video games, and DVDs. Behind it all is a grown man whose personality has often been compared to his creation, the juvenile prankster Bart Simpson.

Although Groening describes himself as "a writer who just happens to be a cartoonist"[1] he has used his writing and drawing talents to transform worldwide culture. People from Argentina to New Zealand are as familiar with the animated Simpson family as they are with living sports heroes, politicians, and celebrities. When British citizens were asked in a 2007 online survey to name the Americans they most admired, the supreme goof-off Homer Simpson ranked higher than Abraham Lincoln and Martin Luther King Jr.

Groening's talents have made him a multimillionaire, but his roots can be traced to a humble middle-class family in Portland, Oregon. Groening learned cartooning from his father and used his artistic talents to help him cope with school. As Groening wrote:

> I've been a drawer of curves and ovals and squiggly lines for as long as I can remember. I can even pinpoint the moment when my fate as a lifelong compulsive doodler was sealed: The first day of first grade. That's when I began to draw, and draw and draw and draw, on whatever surface and with whatever tool I had handy. Why? Because I found school so unbelievably boring that I had to do something—anything—to keep myself from going out of my mind.[2]

Groening was obsessed with cartooning by the time he graduated college. After moving to Los Angeles in 1977, he used his wicked wit and crude drawings to take on the geeks, phonies, show-offs, and incompetent businessmen he encountered while working a series of menial jobs. He self-published his first comic book, *Life in Hell*, and sold it for two dollars at punk rock record stores.

When Groening created *The Simpsons* in 1987, he incorporated the scathing social commentary of *Life in Hell* into his new project. However, the immediate success of the show can be traced to Groening's love of the "everyman," the ordinary person who struggles with money, work, and family issues. Like real people, the *Simpsons* characters can be lazy, jealous, mean, and conniving, but they are also big-hearted, funny, insecure, and sympathetic.

> "I've been a drawer of curves and ovals and squiggly lines for as long as I can remember."[2]
>
> —Matt Groening, cocreator of *The Simpsons*.

Recognizable Characters

The Simpsons was immediately successful because so many people related to the rebellious and perceptive Bart. The personalities of Bart's know-it-all sister, Lisa, his well-meaning mother, Marge, and his clueless father, Homer, were also instantly recognizable. Groening created other iconic *Simpsons* characters like the bully Nelson Muntz, the evil CEO Mr. Burns, and the nerdy Comic Book Guy. All gave Groening a platform from which to gently mock, satirize, criticize, and sometimes celebrate American culture.

Like *The Simpsons*, *Futurama* was designed to mock the present day—but it takes place in the thirty-first century. With Groening at the helm, *Futurama* characters are similar in many ways to those in *The Simpsons*. *Futurama*'s lead character, Philip J. Fry, might be a vision of a twenty-year-old Bart Simpson. Fry is a lowly pizza delivery boy who cannot do anything right and is looking toward a life filled with failure. Fry's love interest, Leela, with a purple ponytail as long as Marge Simpson's piled-up blue hair, is the thirty-first-century mother type. Like Marge, Leela is always acting as the responsible one trying to reign in the show's nutty characters.

Your Authorities Are Goofballs

With the overwhelming popularity of *The Simpsons* and *Futurama*, the shows have attracted some of the biggest celebrities in the world to lend their voices and caricatures to the show. Those who have done

Matt Groening, the award-winning creator of The Simpsons, *celebrates one of the many anniversaries of his popular animated television series beside life-sized versions of his popular characters (from left, Lisa, Maggie, Homer, and Bart Simpson).*

voice acting on the shows include rock stars such as Justin Bieber, Lady Gaga, Katy Perry, former Beatle Paul McCartney, and the White Stripes. Guest-shot rappers include Snoop Dogg, Sir Mix-a-Lot, and 50 Cent. The show has also featured an array of Hollywood superstars such as Reese Witherspoon, Ben Stiller, Zooey Deschanel, Joe Mantegna, and Paul Newman. Even renowned astrophysicist Stephen Hawking, former vice-president Al Gore, and British prime minister Tony Blair have lent their voices to Groening's cartoon stand-ins.

When he created *The Simpsons*, Groening said that he watched so much bad TV as a kid that he wanted to seek revenge by creating a twisted sitcom about a typical American family. According to Groening, his message was, "Your moral authorities don't always have your best interests in mind. Teachers, principals, clergymen, politicians—for the Simpsons, they're all goofballs, and I think that's a great message for kids."[3]

> "Your moral authorities don't always have your best interests in mind."[3]
>
> —Matt Groening, cocreator of *The Simpsons*.

By 2014 *The Simpsons* had won dozens of awards, including thirty-one Primetime Emmy Awards, thirty Annie Awards, and a Peabody Award. While mocking American society, the show rose to the pinnacle of pop culture. In today's fractured media world, with many alternatives to network TV, perhaps it is unlikely that any other show will have as much widespread significance as *The Simpsons*. But Matt Groening's place in television history is secure as a writer who just happens to be a cartoonist who just happened to create the most influential show in television history.

CHAPTER ONE

Growing Up Groening

Matthew Abram "Matt" Groening was born February 15, 1954, in Portland, Oregon. His family name, *Groening* (GRAY-ning), rhymes with *complaining*, as he likes to point out. Groening was the middle child of five, and his parents and siblings provided names for future Simpson characters. His father, Homer, and his mother, Margaret or Marge, lent their names to the Simpson family parents. Margaret Groening's maiden name, Wiggum, was given to Clancy Wiggum, the police chief in the Simpsons' hometown of Springfield. Bart Simpson's siblings were named after two of Groening's sisters, Maggie and Lisa.

Groening's third sister, Patty, provided a name for one of Bart's aunts—Patty Bouvier, the younger of Marge Simpson's chain-smoking twin sisters. However, there was no Bart Groening. The name *Bart* was created by Groening rearranging the letters of the word *brat*. But the Groening family did live on a long, winding road called Evergreen Terrace, the name of the street the Simpsons live on.

Award-Winning Writer

Margaret Groening was a high school English teacher. Homer Groening was an advertising executive who also drew cartoons and made films. In 1964 Homer made a short film, *The Story*, starring Matt and Lisa. The young brother and sister were shown walking through misty fields, holding a garden snake, and visiting an elephant at the zoo.

The Story was based on a tale Matt made up about a brother and sister having an adventure in the woods with some animals. Homer Groening often tape-recorded his family in secret when they were driving in the car or having dinner. Matt told the story to Lisa, who told it to Maggie. The tape recording of Lisa reciting Matt's story provides the soundtrack to the movie. Several years after it was shot,

The Story was shown at a local movie theater, giving Matt his first exposure on the big screen.

Homer Groening's interest in cartooning led him to subscribe to popular magazines like *New Yorker* and *Punch*, famous for their sophisticated cartoons. Matt Groening recalls looking at cartoon drawings even before he could read. And since his father was an artist, sketch pads and marker pens were always available. Groening soon started doodling, with his father's encouragement. According to Groening, this set him on his life's path: "I always knew I was going to be drawing cartoons. I was greatly influenced by my father."[4]

By the time he was eight years old, Groening was drawing cartoon characters such as Charlie Brown from the still-popular daily comic strip *Peanuts*. Groening also wrote short stories. In third grade he briefly attracted national attention when he won a contest held by *Jack and Jill* magazine. It was a finish-the-story contest in which young writers were asked to create a short story based on a few opening sentences supplied by the magazine.

The *Jack and Jill* tale began with a small boy who climbed up into the attic on Halloween and bumped his head on some rafters. After receiving the blow, the boy said, "Now I know what I want to be. . . ." Groening describes his story: "Most kids wrote 'I wanna be a cowboy,' or 'a fireman.' In mine, the kid struck his head and he died and they boarded up the attic and every year on Halloween he'd come down and eat dinner in silence with his family and then go back up to the attic."[5]

> "I always knew I was going to be drawing cartoons. I was greatly influenced by my father."[4]
>
> —Matt Groening, cocreator of *The Simpsons*.

While Groening could tell a good story, sometimes his words got him into trouble with the neighborhood bullies. In fourth grade he enraged an older boy by using big words that the bully did not understand. In a scene reminiscent of *The Simpsons*, Groening was warned that he would be beat up after school. When the time came, Groening picked one boy to hit as hard as he could. The rest of the bullies jumped in and gave Groening a beating. Despite the fact that Groening threw the first punch, the bullies were all forced to apologize to him in the principal's office the next day.

Matt Groening named many of the characters in The Simpsons *after family members. Among them is Springfield police chief Clancy Wiggum. Wiggum is the maiden name of Groening's mother.*

Keeping Track of His Troubles

Groening was in the Boy Scouts by the time he was twelve, when his interest in the written word got him in trouble. On one occasion he was staying in a hotel room on his way to a Boy Scout camping trip. He stole a Gideon's Bible from the hotel and underlined all the parts he considered racy. When a scoutmaster found the defaced Bible, Groening was thrown out of the troop. He later recorded his feelings about the Boy

Scouts in a diary he kept at the time: "The Boy Scouts are alright if you don't have much to do, or you like to pretend to be in the army, and you enjoy saluting the flag, but if all you're in for is because you like camping or your parents make you go, then there's not much to say for it."[6]

Groening later said he kept a diary so he could keep a record of all the times he got in trouble. Even as a boy, Groening knew he would want to look up his misdeeds in the future so he could decide whether he was right or wrong. Diary entries included a run-in with police for riding on a railroad flatcar and an episode in which he threw an encyclopedia out the window of his classroom. Groening also recorded the punishments he received. When he was reprimanded for making wisecracks in class, the teacher made him write five hundred times in a notebook, "I must remember to be quiet in class."[7] This inspired the opening credits for *The Simpsons* in which Bart is shown at a classroom chalkboard writing funny phrases like "I will not burp in class" and "I will not hide the teacher's medication"[8] that give clues to the range of his misdeeds.

Because of his rebellious nature, Groening has one overriding childhood memory: sitting on the bench outside the principal's office. While waiting to be reprimanded, he vowed he would someday make up for all the time adults made him waste. Unlike Bart Simpson, however, Groening was a good student who was popular and achieved decent grades despite his rebelliousness. The main thing that worried his mother was that he spent too much time alone in his room drawing cartoons and listening to rock music.

The Electric Puppy

Like most other kids, Groening loved television; he once said that the story of his childhood could be written by reading old *TV Guide* program schedules. Groening recalled that as a child he watched *The Flintstones* cartoon every Wednesday at 7:30 p.m.

The Flintstones, on the air from 1960 to 1966, was enormously popular. It was the first animated show to run on television during prime time—the hours between 7:00 and 10:00 p.m. *The Flintstones* featured a typical suburban family, except this family lived in the Stone Age. The family consisted of father Fred Flintstone, mother Wilma, and daughter Pebbles. Groening's love of *The Flintstones* would provide inspiration for *The Simpsons*.

Watching cartoons provided Groening with vivid dreams filled with animated characters. Groening recalled one childhood dream that illuminated the peculiar mixture of cuteness, humor, and mortal fear that guided his later work. Groening's dream featured a loving little dog named Electric Puppy. As Groening tells it, there was a "cartoon puppy—the happiest, friendliest puppy, who just wants to love and be loved by everyone. But he has a lightning bolt for a tail. And if he touches you, you die. My brother and I were riding our bicycles, and the puppy was romping after us, and we're going, 'Yes! Good puppy! But don't kill us!'"[9]

In grade school Groening's colorful imagination inspired him to form the Creature Club with other artistic friends. The motto of the group was "I'm Peculiar." The other kids in the Creature Club drew superheroes that looked like Batman. But Groening could not draw muscle-bound crusaders because he lacked that type of artistic skill. Instead he drew pictures of animals. But even these cartoons were so bad that no one could figure out what the characters were supposed to be. People thought Groening's drawing of an owl was a little bear. In order to make his animal drawing more recognizable, Groening added long ears and named his creation Rotten Rabbit. This character became the inspiration for Binky the Rabbit, which would later appear in Groening's *Life in Hell* comic strip.

The First Bart Simpson

After Groening entered Lincoln High School in 1969, he produced another memorable character that would eventually take on a life of its own. While trying to write a novel, Groening invented a character named Bart Simpson. Groening provides details of the story:

> I thought it was a very unusual name for a kid at the time. I had this idea of an angry father yelling "Bart," and Bart sounds kind of like bark—like a barking dog. I thought it would sound funny. In my novel, Bart was the son of Homer Simpson. . . . I thought Simpson was a funny name in that it had the word "simp" in it, which is short for "simpleton"—I just went with it.[10]

A Strong Sense of Self-Pity

Like Bart Simpson, Matt Groening was an unruly student who once got in trouble in class for making high-pitched meowing noises like a sick cat. In a 1986 interview, Groening recalled the Bart-like ways he used to torment his teachers and sisters:

> When I was a kid I had a strong sense of bitterness and self-pity and all that stuff. I got in trouble quite a lot when I was a kid. . . . I mouthed off to the teachers quite a bit, and I got in trouble. Got sent to the corner quite a bit for everything. When I was at the corner, I learned a new little talent—I took a bit of string and learned how to make a hangman's noose, which got me into further trouble, and sent me to the corner again. Then I learned to blow bubbles off the end of my tongue, a skill which I tormented my sister[s] with again and again. To this day I can get them to scream doing it.

Quoted in Richard von Busack, "'Life' Before Homer," Metroactive, 2000. www.metroactive.com.

Groening's teachers recognized his writing talents and appointed him editor of the high school newspaper. However, the cartoons he contributed ridiculed teachers, prom queens, and football players. He was eventually fired.

Teens for Decency

Groening's high school years coincided with the counterculture revolution that was shaking up American society. Millions of young people were becoming hippies, rejecting mainstream culture, listening to acid rock, and watching experimental "underground" movies.

Like many other American males of the era, Groening grew long hair and became a hippie. He also became politically aware, joining in protests against the US involvement in the Vietnam War. However, while some protesters were calling for a violent revolution, Groening relied on his sense of humor to ridicule the political and social climate.

Groening formed a joke political party at school called Teens for Decency. In an event that sounds very much like a *Simpsons* episode, Groening ran for student body president on the motto "If You're Against Decency, What Are You For?"[11] The slogan confused students who did not get the joke. They overwhelmingly elected Groening, but he regretted his victory immediately. He was not interested in presiding over the student body; he only wanted to make fun of the straitlaced, Lisa Simpson–type kids who typically populated student government.

Young, long-haired protesters rally against the Vietnam War in Washington, DC, in 1971. Groening grew his hair long and joined in antiwar protests during the 1960s and early 1970s.

Groening's quirky sense of humor carried over to his after-school job working in the kitchen at a convalescent home called Kearney Care Center. Many of the elderly patients at the care center had lost their teeth over the years. Groening's childhood friend, Richard Gehr, worked alongside him in the kitchen. Gehr comments, "I remember Matt saying the motto for the place should be 'you can eat what you choose, but you can't chew what you eat.'"[12] The job undoubtedly provided inspiration for *The Simpsons'* Springfield Retirement Castle, home to Abe "Grandpa" Simpson. Bart and Lisa both put in time working at the Springfield Retirement Castle.

"Is It Worth Doing?"

When it was time to go to college, Groening applied to Harvard University but was relieved when he was accepted at Evergreen State College in Olympia, Washington. Evergreen was known for its liberal, unstructured policies; there were no grades and no core requirements. Teachers encouraged creativity, and it was not necessary for students to declare a major. This was a perfect fit for Groening, who swore at his high school graduation he would never take another test.

Study programs at Evergreen were arranged so that students focused on one subject, six hours a day, for the entire semester. Groening decided to study under the most demanding teacher on campus, Mark Levensky, who taught philosophy and fiction writing. Groening wrote numerous short stories for the class. At the end of the semester, according to Groening, Levensky made a comment that left a permanent mark on him: "He drew a formula on the blackboard that described the plot of every one of my short stories. It was a pretty simple formula. And then he said, 'You do what you do fairly well. Now you have to ask yourself, is it worth doing?' And that's haunted me for the rest of my life. That is the question that I keep asking myself."[13]

Groening's writing talents, though, earned him a job as editor of the Evergreen student newspaper, the *Cooper Point Journal*. Even among the hippies working on the paper, Groening managed to stand out. When he was working against a deadline and did not want to be disturbed, he wrapped a piece of wire around his head so there was an antenna sticking up. The wire antenna was Groening's signal that he did not want anyone to bother him.

Evergreen Flakes

Groening created scathing comics for the *Cooper Point Journal*, and some generated extremely negative letters to the editor. Groening was often seen with his head in his hands, wondering if he had gone too far in attacking the overly sincere progressives at school. One of his cartoons created a campus uproar. The cartoon showed a cereal box with the words "Evergreen Flakes" on the front. It pictured a group of hippies sitting around a bowl labeled "leisure cereal of the state of Washington." The caption read, "Achievement Without Effort."[14]

Groening expected the cartoon to create howls of laughter among the student body while offending the faculty. Instead the students were hurt but teachers thought Groening was hilarious. The cartoon, ridiculing lazy students, was pinned up on classroom walls and bulletin boards throughout the campus. One student, Terry Wright, even wrote a letter to Groening thanking him for making the *Cooper Point Journal* so bad. Wright said this would leave him more time for his studies because he would never have to spend another minute reading the paper.

> "[Matt] was always surprised and sad and a bit worried that [his cartoons] would affect his peers in such a negative fashion."[16]
>
> —Leo Daugherty, literary professor and Matt Groening's mentor.

Another Groening cartoon made fun of city hippies who moved to rural communes to grow their own food and share possessions and chores. This one prompted readers to draft a protest petition that was eventually signed by one hundred students. It said, "Dear Mr. Groening: Communal struggles are not funny!"[15]

While some social commentators love taunting their pompous targets, Groening was upset by the criticism. As Evergreen literary professor and Groening mentor Leo Daugherty recalls: "[Matt] was always surprised and sad and a bit worried that [his cartoons]

"Learn and Have a Good Time"

In June 2000 Matt Groening returned to his alma mater, Evergreen State College in Olympia, Washington, to deliver the commencement speech at graduation. An article from the *Seattle Times*, written by reporter Mark Rahner, describes Groening as he prepared for the occasion:

> Bart Simpson would never be allowed inside a college.
>
> But Matt Groening, creator of "The Simpsons" who has built an empire on ridiculing authority figures, will stand behind the lectern today as the commencement speaker at his alma mater, The Evergreen State College. . . .
>
> "I left in shame, and now I'm returning in triumph," he said in a phone call from his Los Angeles office. "Well, I don't know if I left in shame, but I was kind of ashamed.". . .
>
> He admitted he'd put off writing his speech "like it's the final term paper I never finished." But there were some pearls of wisdom he could have used at his own graduation: "It's always good to have a good enough friend whose couch you can sleep on when you get evicted. And wash the dishes at the house that you're crashing at, and they'll be less inclined to kick you out."
>
> "Evergreen was a blast," Groening recalled. "Kids spend their late adolescence rebelling against authority, if they've got any gumption. But there's nothing to rebel against at Evergreen, so you thrash about a bit at first, and then you go, 'Oh, wait, I'm here to learn and have a good time.'"

Mark Rahner, "Matt Groening to Give Grads Bart-like Wisdom?," *Seattle Times*, June 9, 2000. http://community.seattletimes.nwsource.com.

would affect his peers in such a negative fashion. I could tell a mile away when Matt had had one of his run-ins. But I always looked forward to the ensuing conversation, because I knew it would be interesting."[16]

Although Groening could not have known it, the college controversies were a projection of things to come. During the first few seasons of *The Simpsons*, Groening was widely criticized for damaging the self-esteem of adolescents and undermining American values.

"A Guy with Real Strong Feelings"

When Groening was at a low point, questioning his cartooning abilities, he was fortunate to meet future cartoonist Lynda Barry. Groening explains, "She was this crazy girl who did the wildest cartoons I'd

Longtime friends Matt Groening and cartoonist Lynda Barry enjoy favorite cartoon clips during a lecture in Chicago, Illinois. The two met early in their careers, at a time when Groening was questioning his cartooning abilities.

ever seen and was very inspiring to me. She showed me you could do cartoons about anything."[17]

Although Barry is most widely known for her weekly comic strip *Ernie Pook's Comeek*, she is also a playwright, novelist, and teacher. Groening first heard about her at Evergreen after she wrote a gag letter to the renowned author of *Catch-22*, Joseph Heller. Barry asked Heller to marry her, and the author actually wrote her back. Heller said he had to decline her offer because he did not want to live in a college dormitory. Groening thought Barry's prank was great, so he hired her to write stories for the *Cooper Point Journal*. Her first offering was a dark comedy called "Thanksgiving for One."

At the time Groening met Barry, most cartoons published in newspapers and magazines were stale and predictable. Comic strips like *Blondie*, *Gasoline Alley*, and *Beetle Bailey* had been around for decades and were never controversial. However, they were all drawn by skilled artists.

> "[Matt Groening is] a guy with real strong feelings, and in his cartoons . . . he's found a way to make strong feelings and sad feelings about families work."[18]
>
> —Lynda Barry, cartoonist and author.

Groening could not draw well, and he did not see anything in the commercial marketplace that looked like his work. Barry convinced Groening his work was worthwhile. In return, Groening encouraged Barry, who was a painter at the time, to consider cartooning.

In 1990 Barry was asked about her time at Evergreen. She recalled there were so many weird hippies at the school that Groening looked straight by comparison, "but so militantly straight that he was hipper than the hippies. He was . . . a guy with real strong feelings, and in his cartoons, and now 'The Simpsons,' he's found a way to make strong feelings and sad feelings about families work."[18] Barry also noted that Groening was known for winning arguments with his stinging comments—or what she called his "battery-acid tongue."[19]

Overdoing It

There is little doubt that millions of people identify with Groening's school experiences, but while many suffer through bullying, rejection,

> ## "Don't do it. Overdo it."[20]
> —Homer Groening, Matt's father.

and insecurity in silence, Groening did not. He tapped his creative abilities and turned negative childhood incidents into social commentary and comedy. He was lucky enough to glean inspiration from his father, who provided him with tools to deal with his peculiar view of the world. While Groening has accomplished much in his life, he never backed down or did anything halfway. Perhaps more than anything, Groening's life has been inspired by his father's motto, "Don't do it. Overdo it."[20]

CHAPTER TWO

Life in Hell

The Los Angeles, California, neighborhood known as Hollywood has been at the center of the entertainment industry for more than a century. And for nearly as long, Hollywood has been a magnet for budding writers, actors, directors, and producers.

However, fewer than one in a hundred Hollywood hopefuls ever land a job in the entertainment business. But the odds against success did not deter Matt Groening after he graduated from Evergreen State College in 1977. At age twenty-three, Groening had hopes of becoming a successful writer. He says he moved to Los Angeles "because it was the city in which writers were the most overpaid in the world."[21]

Like many others who seek the glitter and gloss of Hollywood, Groening found it to be quite different from the city portrayed in movies. Los Angeles was filled with run-down apartments, terrible traffic, and choking air pollution. When Groening first arrived the temperature was a scorching 102°F (39°C), and his 1972 Datsun immediately broke down in the fast lane of the Hollywood Freeway. Then things got worse.

The Writer/Chauffeur

With no idea how to break into the publishing or entertainment business, Groening began a futile search for any type of work. At one point he was so desperate for money that he hunted for lost change in the bright orange shag carpeting of his dingy Hollywood apartment. As Groening recalls, "It was the most miserable time of my life. Heartbreak is light and lively compared to unemployment."[22]

Groening finally spotted a want ad in the newspaper seeking the services of a writer/chauffeur. Excited by the prospect of a writing job, Groening applied and was hired. The position was offered by an

At the age of twenty-three, Groening moved to smoggy, traffic-filled Los Angeles, California (pictured). He had hopes of making it big as a writer in Los Angeles but without a job his first months there were mostly miserable.

eighty-eight-year-old man who had once directed cheap, grade-B Westerns. During the day Groening performed his chauffeur duties. He drove the man around the wealthy neighborhood of Beverly Hills, which was home to many movie stars. As Groening describes it, the elderly man was often confused when remembering long-dead stars like Cary Grant and the comedy team of Stan Laurel and Oliver Hardy: "Unfortunately, he was losing his mind. I'd drive him through Beverly Hills, and we'd see a house, and he'd say 'Oh, there's Cary Grant's house. Boy, the parties we'd have,' and then he'd reminisce and drift off into a story. Then the next day, we'd be driving by the same house, and he'd say, 'Oh, there's Laurel and Hardy's house. Boy, the parties we'd have.'"[23]

After his driving duties were finished for the day, Groening performed his writing chores. He sat in the director's living room and added to the thousand-page manuscript compiled by other writer/chauffeurs previously employed by the man. When Groening pointed out to the director that Laurel and Hardy worked together but never lived in the same house, he was fired.

Binky, Bongo, and Sheba

Groening finally found steady work at a Hollywood copy shop, where he had access to plenty of paper and marking pens. During slow hours Groening drew cartoon characters and wrote out thoughts about his lonely, desperate life. His scribbling evolved into a comic strip. He chose a title he felt most accurately reflected his Hollywood experience, *Life in Hell*. Groening created the strip as an alternative to writing long, depressing letters to friends and family back in the Pacific Northwest. He ran off copies of the strip at work and mailed them home as a way to keep in touch.

Groening's comic starred Binky, a bulgy-eyed rabbit with a massive overbite. Groening said he called the character Binky because it was the stupidest name he could think of. Other *Life in Hell* characters included Bongo, Binky's son, and Sheba, Binky's irritable girlfriend.

Bongo was born out of wedlock, a product of Binky's chance encounter with a stranger in a singles bar. The story was featured in an early *Life in Hell* strip called "Jungle Passion." Bongo, who always seemed to be fearful and panicked, only had one ear. Groening freely admits that his drawing skills were so limited that he gave Bongo the single ear so that viewers could tell him apart from Binky. Groening also admits that Sheba was simply a drawing of Binky but wearing a dress, a bow, and a pearl necklace. The necklace would later appear on both Marge and Lisa Simpson. Binky and Bongo dolls would show up on *The Simpsons* as toys for Bart, Lisa, and Maggie.

Working at Licorice Pizza

In 1978 Groening landed a job at the Licorice Pizza record store on Hollywood's famed Sunset Boulevard. Licorice Pizza was at the center of the exploding Los Angeles punk rock music scene in the late 1970s. In this era before the Internet, independent Los Angeles punk bands like X, the Deadbeats, and the Germs were known for their do-it-yourself methods of promotion. Unlike the rock supergroups of the era, which earned millions recording for multinational record companies, punk bands sold their music at stores like Licorice Pizza on cheap, self-made cassette tapes. The bands promoted their music with fan magazines, or fanzines, with names like *Slash*, *Flipside*, and *Starting Fires*.

Groening found inspiration in both the punk rock music and the fanzines that he sold in the record store. Since he had piles of *Life in Hell* do-it-yourself comic books from his time at the copy shop, Groening placed them in the punk rock section of Licorice Pizza. He sold copies for two dollars.

Working at the *Reader*

In 1978 Groening managed to get *Life in Hell* published for the first time, in a monthly publication called *Wet: The Magazine of Gourmet Bathing*. The magazine did not really cover bathing. *Wet* featured experimental artwork, articles on the environment and punk culture, and *Life in Hell* comic strips.

Groening's situation continued to improve when he got a job at another new publication, the *Los Angeles Reader*. The paper was a free alternative newspaper that covered music, art, film, theater, and cultural events. During his job interview with *Reader* editor James Vowell, Groening showed off copies of *Life in Hell*. According to Groening, Vowell "hired me immediately—to deliver newspapers."[24]

The Los Angeles Punk Scene

In the early 1980s punk music, art, and fashion were blossoming in Los Angeles. The alternative weekly *Los Angeles Reader,* where Groening was employed, was one of the few papers covering the punk explosion in the city. Gary Panter, known as the "father of punk comics," was Groening's close friend and coworker. Panter describes the scene:

> Punk rock was happening, so there were shows all the time. And Matt and me and everybody went to these shows. And a lot of the same bands would play, they became very famous, and it was really creative. Punk rock in LA was a lot of people out of art school, doing creative things, making publications and clothing and music and so on. We were part of that. And the idea that we could get things into the *LA Reader* and then have [the crumpled up newspaper pages] blowing down the street, weeks later, seem like some sort of interesting accomplishment, to impact the landscape somehow. And I think Matt and I were both interested in doing that. We were both interested in entering into culture somehow. It's interesting if the individual can have an effect on culture.

Quoted in John Ortved, *The Simpsons: An Uncensored, Unauthorized History.* New York: Faber and Faber, 2009, p. 18.

Groening's official title was circulation manager. The job involved using his beat-up 1962 Ford Fairlane to deliver heavy bundles of newspapers to convenience stores, bars, liquor marts, and record shops. Groening also performed numerous other jobs at the newly founded newspaper, including answering phones, writing headlines, editing, and proofreading.

Vowell soon let Groening write short articles for the paper and conduct interviews with rock musicians such as Elvis Costello and Talking Heads lead singer David Byrne. As a rock writer for an alternative weekly, Groening visited the trendiest clubs in Los Angeles with his coworkers, where they saw the hottest bands. As *Reader* publisher Jane Levine recalls: "[It was] this totally fun time in L.A. The late seventies, early eighties. Punk rock. And . . . this little group of us [published a paper] and hung out together. You know, we worked a million hours a week, and the hours we weren't working, we hung out together."[25]

While working at a delivery job for the Los Angeles Reader *Groening also wrote short articles about rock stars. Some of the musicians he interviewed later appeared on* The Simpsons, *as in this 2002 episode featuring (from left) Elvis Costello, Tom Petty, Keith Richards, Homer Simpson, Mick Jagger, Lenny Kravitz, and Brian Setzer.*

During long, all-night work sessions on the paper, Groening and Vowell often ate at a local diner. This exclusive time with Vowell provided Groening with an opportunity to sell *Life in Hell* to the editor. Groening would crack jokes and make comical Binky and Bongo drawings on paper napkins. Vowell was impressed by the strip, but Levine says she was skeptical: "Matt came in with these silly cartoons with the rabbit with one ear. And showed them to James ... [who] says 'That guy is gonna be famous some day.' And I look at these flipping rabbits, you know, and go, 'Whatever James.'"[26]

Despite Levine's misgivings, Vowell decided to run the strip. *Life in Hell* first appeared in the *Reader* on April 25, 1980. Vowell commented on Groening's talents: "He would practice drawing those characters all the time, thinking carefully and meticulously about how to get the exact line stroke that looks casual but is completely repeatable. I actually think the drawings are exquisitely well done."[27]

> "[Matt Groening] would practice drawing those characters all the time, thinking carefully and meticulously about how to get the exact line stroke."[27]
>
> —James Vowell, editor of the *Los Angeles Reader*.

Akbar and Jeff

Although it may be hard to believe in the twenty-first century, the title Groening chose for his strip was considered controversial in the early 1980s. The word *hell* was almost unprintable at the time and was rarely heard on TV. *Hell* was considered a curse word, and its use offended some religious conservatives. When asked about the controversy, Groening stated that he was agnostic, someone who believes that nothing is known or can be known of the existence of God. However, Groening joked that he did come to believe in hell after viewing some of the awful programs that appeared on prime-time television.

In addition to the comic's title, Groening added several characters that were considered provocative. Akbar and Jeff were fez-wearing gay midgets who looked, acted, and thought alike. The two had an intense love-hate relationship but were supersalesmen who could market any product. Their businesses included Akbar & Jeff's Tofu Hut and Akbar & Jeff's Earthquake T-Shirt Hut.

Groening based Akbar and Jeff on the popular Muppet characters Bert and Ernie, who appeared in the children's television show *Sesame Street*. But in the socially conservative 1980s, gay people were often publically denounced by prominent politicians and religious leaders. According to NPR correspondent Glen Weldon, in this environment Akbar and Jeff "were, weirdly enough and almost by default, pretty much the most high-profile gay couple of the '80s."[28]

Tormented and Tortured

Drawings of Akbar, Jeff, and the other *Life in Hell* characters mostly served as vehicles for Groening's pointed commentary. In some strips every bit of spare space was packed with lists, moral questions, and eccentric definitions concerning life, love, work, and other topics.

Life in Hell characters also expressed Groening's tortured attitudes. Binky was irritable, preachy, cranky, paranoid, and snide. In the early strips the self-centered Binky was solely focused on his own pain. He was fearful he was having a nervous breakdown, troubled by the sounds of gunshots and sirens late at night, and queasy from the brown, polluted air. His tragic attempts to find love left him questioning his very existence.

In one strip Binky explained the meaning of life to Bongo, which also summed up Groening's outlook at the time: "You're afraid there's no heaven. But look on the bright side—there's no hell, either. Except this one. . . . No matter who you are, you gotta die. And we all get to be dead the same amount of time: forever."[29]

> "The more I tortured [my characters], the more the readers loved me."[30]
>
> —Matt Groening, cocreator of *The Simpsons.*

Life in Hell often rehashed Groening's early family life with strip titles such as "Lies My Older Brother and Sister Told Me," and "Lies I Told My Younger Sisters." The strip called "Parent's Guide to Teenage Crime & Punishment" was obviously inspired by the misdeeds and punishments Groening listed in his adolescent diary. Bongo often acted as a stand-in for Groening. The one-eared character was punished in school, ignored by adults, and harassed by bullies.

The *Life in Hell* characters were tormented by love, death, and life in general. But Groening also made it clear they were victimized by outside forces such as bosses, religious leaders, conservative politicians, and greedy corporations. This made *Life in Hell* seem more relevant to the young, comic-reading public. According to Groening, "The more I tortured [my characters], the more the readers loved me."[30]

Two of the characters in Groening's first successful newspaper cartoon strip, Life in Hell, *were based on the popular* Sesame Street *Muppets, Ernie (left) and Bert. But Groening's two characters were fez-wearing gay midgets who looked, acted, and thought alike.*

"I Hate Everything"

Binky's growing popularity prompted the *Reader* to give Groening a weekly music column called Sound Mix. The column was supposed to feature music-scene gossip, but Groening was not interested in idle chatter concerning rock musicians. Instead, he used Sound Mix to describe his petty grievances, his work life, and his childhood.

One Sound Mix column was called "Tales of the Beaver Patrol: My Life in the Boy Scouts." Another described the war he was waging against his noisy neighbor who played drums in the apartment downstairs. Groening sometimes filled his Sound Mix column in much the same way he packed the margins of *Life in Hell*. He made lists of thing he liked. For example, Groening liked underground comics and a book called *The American Thesaurus of Slang*. Sometimes he veered off into things he hated: "*Style*. Both the word and the concept. And the word yuppie. Also what I'm getting paid to write this. Also this bad cold I have. I hate everything."[31]

When he had nothing else to write about, Groening would invent bands and write reviews of their nonexistent records. The next week Groening would admit that he made up the band and promise that everything in the current column was absolutely true. It was not. Vowell was not amused by such pranks, and Groening was soon asked to give up the Sound Mix column.

"Quit Your Lousy Job"

While working at the *Reader*, Groening met Deborah Caplan, a sales representative for the paper. Caplan's job involved visiting businesses such as clothing stores and bars and convincing owners to advertise in the *Reader*. According to Caplan, she quickly came to appreciate how *Life in Hell* made her job easier: "It didn't take many sales calls before I realized that Groening's comic strip was the major drawing card [attraction] of the newspaper."[32]

Caplan often stated that she was a born salesperson; her father was a Los Angeles car salesman and her mother was a real estate agent. And Caplan was so good at her job that she was soon promoted to sales manager, overseeing a small staff of salespeople. However, Caplan wanted to go into business for herself. She decided to become an artist's representative, and she signed Groening as her first artist. Before long Groening and Caplan were dating.

In November 1984 Caplan helped Groening self-publish a book called *Love Is Hell*. It features a series of *Life in Hell* strips about relationships that had previously appeared in the *Reader*. Caplan had two thousand copies of the book printed, feeling it would be only a minor success during the Christmas shopping season. When *Love Is Hell* sold out in a matter of days, Caplan ordered twenty thousand copies for a second edition, which also sold out.

> "It didn't take many sales calls before I realized that Groening's comic strip was the major drawing card of the newspaper."[32]
>
> —Deborah Caplan, sales manager at the *Los Angeles Reader*.

In 1985, inspired by the *Life in Hell* strip called "Isn't It About Time You Quit Your Lousy Job?," Caplan and Groening quit working at the *Reader*. Together they founded a company called Life in Hell Inc. It sold *Life in Hell* merchandise such as posters, calendars, T-shirts, greeting cards, and coffee mugs. The couple also set up Acme Features Syndicate, a company dedicated to getting *Life in Hell* published throughout the country in as many alternative newspapers as possible. In addition to Groening's work, Acme also handled comic strips by Lynda Barry and other alternative cartoonists.

An Amazing Time

Groening and Caplan moved in together and ran Acme and Life in Hell Inc. out of their kitchen. As Caplan recalls, "It was a blast. I did *all* the business, and Matt just got to be the artist, the struggling artist. And it was a very romantic time for everybody. . . . You know, it was just a really amazing time."[33]

Life in Hell was soon appearing in nearly one hundred papers every week. Each paper only paid fifteen dollars per week to run the strip. But Caplan negotiated a deal for the papers to provide free advertising for *Life in Hell* merchandise. This allowed her to set up a mail-order business to sell *Life in Hell* products to fans across the country.

Binky's Topsy-Turvy World

In 1989 *Washington Post* columnist Richard Harrington reviewed Matt Groening's book *Childhood Is Hell,* a collection of *Life in Hell* comic strips that had previously appeared in alternative newspapers. Harrington wrote:

It's a topsy-turvy world in which lovers and friends can't be trusted, parents are out of control, kids are uncontrollable, students are terrorized by peers and teachers alike—and where everyone seems to be at the mercy of forces beyond their own ken, looking for answers without any idea what the questions are. It's funny and fatalistic, rude and revealing, touching raw nerves, funny bones, and heartstrings all at the same time. . . .

Binky and company don't actually have much personality on their own and they are more appalling than appealing. Mostly they talk, ruminate, whine, advise, and worry; they're mouthpieces for Groening's wired barbs. . . . And they don't sleep well at night. It's the human condition revealed by rabbits. The strips are community mirrors—look in there and you'll see not only yourself, but all too many of the people you know.

Richard Harrington, "Groening Draws on Humor of Life," *Washington Post,* February 12, 1989, p. E14.

By 1986 Life in Hell Inc. was booming. Caplan and Groening published a second book of previously released strips, *Work Is Hell.* To promote the book, Groening toured the country, signing copies at bookstores for his fans. According to Caplan, "Matt was an amazing creative talent . . . but I got to make him famous."[34] She also got to make him her husband. Caplan and Groening were married in 1987.

Beer and Computers

Caplan went on to publish one *Life in Hell* book a year, with titles such as *School Is Hell* (1987), *Childhood Is Hell* (1988), and *Akbar and Jeff's Guide to Life* (1989). The books received numerous positive reviews in major newspapers like the *New York Times* and the *Washington Post*. By 1989 *Life in Hell* was appearing in about three hundred alternative weeklies. Since each paper had from fifty thousand to five hundred thousand readers, Groening felt that he had millions of fans.

Groening's status as an alternative comic artist was very attractive to several major corporations. In 1989 Apple hired Groening to create a series of illustrations for a student guide to Macintosh computers. The cover featured Bongo sitting between high stacks of paper with a headline that read, "Who Needs a Computer Anyway?"[35] Inside the brochure, Groening created cartoon characters he thought represented typical college kids. They had names like "The Procrastinator," "The Imperfectionist," "The Technoid," and "The Unemployed." The brochure, which was distributed at college bookstores, was meant to attract hip young buyers new to computers.

In the early 1990s a major brewing company took an interest in *Life in Hell*. The brewery wanted to use Akbar and Jeff to promote its beer. However, the company did not realize that Akbar and Jeff were gay. Groening picks up the story: "We were [talking] about an Akbar and Jeff spring break train, Akbar and Jeff tattoos, an Akbar and Jeff blimp. We were talking about it very seriously until they read an article on me . . . and found out that Akbar and Jeff had an alternate lifestyle."[36] The company pulled out from the negotiations.

A Thirty-Two-Year Run

By 1989 *Life in Hell* had grown into a thriving industry, and Groening would no longer have to search for coins in the carpeting. The Groenings moved to the trendy Venice Beach neighborhood, and Deborah became pregnant with the couple's first son, Homer. Management of Life in Hell Inc. was handed over to the publishing company Pantheon. At the time, Groening described his work: "'Life in Hell' [is] an ongoing series of self-help cartoons—the self being helped being me. I don't know how helpful these cartoons have been but drawing them over the last ten years has sure amused me. I hope the cartoons amuse you too, but if you're one of those people who finds my stuff annoying, that's OK. Luckily for me, being annoying is a blast, too."[37]

Groening continued to amuse and annoy, drawing *Life in Hell* until June 2012. During the comic's thirty-two-year run, Groening creating a total of 1,669 strips featuring his beloved, if tortured, characters. At the height of the strip's popularity in the 1990's, *Life in Hell* ran in more than 380 papers. However, in the twenty-first century, hundreds of alternative weeklies floundered financially. Free classified advertisement websites like Craigslist deprived papers like the *Reader* of a major source of ad income, and many alternative weeklies ceased publication. By the end of its run, *Life in Hell* was carried in only thirty-eight papers.

> "Groening is modern cartooning's rock god, a Moses who came down from the mountain and handed us the rules we followed."[38]
>
> —Ted Rall, alternative comic strip artist.

Despite the changing scene during its run, *Life in Hell* opened doors for numerous other alternative cartoonists, including Tom Tomorrow, Ward Sutton, and Ted Rall. As Rall wrote after the last *Life in Hell* appeared:

Artistically and creatively, Groening was . . . a huge influence. His primacy of writing over art, a simple, stripped-down drawing style paired with sardonic, dark observations about life . . . the freeform use of interchangeable characters without continuing traits, much less story lines, were the template most of us followed. . . . Groening is modern cartooning's rock god, a Moses who came down from the mountain and handed us the rules we followed.[38]

CHAPTER THREE

The Simpsons Conquer the World

Matt Groening was notorious for not doing his work until the last possible moment. While working at the *Reader*, he often turned in his *Life in Hell* comic strip moments before the issue was set to go to the printers. In typical fashion Groening was totally unprepared in 1986 when he arrived for a very important meeting with James L. Brooks, one of the most successful writers and producers in Hollywood. Brooks was a fan of *Life in Hell* and wanted to produce one-minute animated cartoons featuring the strip's characters. The animations, called bumpers, would be shown before and after commercial breaks on the TV program *The Tracey Ullman Show*. Brooks was producing the show for a new network called the Fox Television Network, or Fox. (The network was later renamed the Fox Broadcasting Company.)

Groening was thrilled to have a meeting with Brooks, but he had a problem using his *Life in Hell* characters. If Fox broadcasted the strip, the network would take partial ownership of Binky, Bongo, Sheba, Akbar, and Jeff. This would give Fox merchandising rights to *Life in Hell* calendars, posters, mugs, and T-shirts.

A Quick Sketch of *The Simpsons*

Groening was not rich, but he made a comfortable living from *Life in Hell*. He was not willing to surrender ownership of his characters to Fox. However, he had arrived in the lobby of Brooks's office with nothing new to show. What happened next is an often-told Hollywood legend. With fifteen minutes to spare before the meeting, Groening quickly sketched out a quirky looking family. It consisted of a father, a mother, two girls, and one boy. For lack of any other names, he called four of the characters Homer, Marge, Lisa, and Maggie after his own family members. The last, Bart Simpson, was the name of a character Groening created in high school.

In the meeting, Brooks and the Fox executives liked what they saw, but they wanted to know a little more. Groening recalls, "They asked me: 'What does the father do?' and I answered, 'He works at a nuclear plant.' They laughed, and then I knew we were in."[39]

The Dark Prince of Comedy

Most struggling Hollywood artists would have been better prepared than Groening when they showed up at Brooks's office. Brooks was a Hollywood legend who began his career in the early 1960s writing some of the top-rated comedy shows on television, including *The Andy Griffith Show* and *My Three Sons*. His success continued in the 1970s when he wrote and produced several award-winning shows such as *The Mary Tyler Moore Show* and *Taxi*. In the 1980s Brooks moved to the big screen, writing, producing, and directing the blockbuster films *Terms of Endearment* and *Broadcast News*.

> "In my mind, if you [are] writing a comedy where human beings experience pain, you're just being realistic."[40]
>
> —James L. Brooks, cocreator of *The Simpsons*.

When Brooks began producing films in the 1980s, his big-hearted characters blended wit, human failings, generosity, neurotic behavior, and tragedy. As Brooks explained to the *Los Angeles Times* in 1993, "In my mind, if you [are] writing a comedy where human beings experience pain, you're just being realistic."[40] Such statements earned Brooks the nickname "the Dark Prince of Comedy." It also helps explain why Brooks was a huge fan of the darkly comedic *Life in Hell*.

The Tracey Ullman Show

In 1986 Brooks created his own production company, Gracie Films. In its way Gracie resembled the alternative weekly newspapers that ran *Life in Hell*. Brooks founded the studio to produce TV shows and

The Simpsons *first appeared on television as one-minute animated shorts on* The Tracey Ullman Show. *The show featured the quirky English comedian Tracey Ullman (pictured in a 1987 episode).*

films that were creative, edgy, and out of the mainstream. These alternative concepts were shunned by large Hollywood studios.

With a new film company, Brooks began searching for original talent. Few performers at the time were quirkier than the English comedian Tracey Ullman. In the early 1980s Ullman launched her

The President Takes On *The Simpsons*

The Simpsons was so popular that the show even caught the attention of highly placed Washington officials. In December 1990 the director of the Office of National Drug Control, "Drug Czar" William Bennett, was visiting a drug rehabilitation center when he noticed a Bart Simpson poster on the wall. Bennett told the recovering addicts, "You guys aren't watching *The Simpsons,* are you? That isn't going to help you any." When asked about the comment by a reporter, Bennett said, "I'll sit down with the little spike head, we'll straighten this thing out. . . . There's nothing that a Catholic school, a paper route, and a couple of soap sandwiches wouldn't straighten out." This inspired a retort from *Simpsons* writers: "If our Drug Czar thinks he can sit down and talk this over with a cartoon character, he must be on something."

Two years later, when President George H.W. Bush was running for re-election, the nation was suffering from an economic recession. In a 1992 speech, Bush invoked the name of *The Waltons,* a popular TV show about a family living in rural Virginia in the 1930s, during the Great Depression. Bush said if he was reelected, he would make families "a lot more like the Waltons and a lot less like the Simpsons." *Simpsons* writers retaliated once again. In an episode showing the Simpsons watching Bush's speech on TV, Bart responds, "We're just like the Waltons. We're praying for an end to the Depression too."

Quoted in John Ortved, *The Simpsons: An Uncensored, Unauthorized History.* New York: Faber and Faber, 2009, p. 122.

career as a rock satirist with an album called *You Broke My Heart in 17 Places*. Ullman's songs mocked the overly produced pop music of the time and featured silly lyrics backed by sugary vocal arrangements.

In addition to singing, Ullman danced and did impressions of famous actors and politicians. Ullman was famous in Great Britain, and in 1986 Brooks joined forces with her to create *The Tracey Ullman Show* for American audiences.

The Tracey Ullman Show was the one of first original series aired on Fox. The show blended short comedy scenes, or sketches, with musical numbers in which Ullman parodied popular songs of the day. With the addition of *The Simpsons* shorts, Brooks felt he was adding something different to help *The Tracey Ullman Show* stand apart from similar shows such as *Saturday Night Live*.

Like other TV variety programs, *The Tracey Ullman Show* was a major production that involved hundreds of people working behind the scenes. Groening's one-minute animated *Simpsons* bumpers were seen by Fox executives as extremely minor additions to the show. When it came time to negotiate the rights to *Simpsons* merchandise, Fox had low expectations. At the time, few TV shows had ever produced merchandise that sold well. Fox allowed Groening to retain a large percentage of possible revenues produced by his characters. Groening was also able to maintain creative control over his creations, deciding how they would be marketed and on what products they would appear.

After the successful meeting at Fox, one of the show executives saw Groening sitting at a bus stop—he did not even own a car at that time. What no one could have realized was that the hurriedly sketched characters Groening had just created would soon be worth billions of dollars.

Designing the Simpsons

Groening created each *Simpsons* character to be recognizable as a silhouette. He gave Homer his big beer belly, Marge her towering beehive hairstyle, and Bart and Lisa their spiky locks. And all the original characters had massive overbites like Binky, Bongo, and Sheba.

The task of turning Groening's cartoon sketches into animated cartoons was given to a small animation company in Hollywood called Klasky Csupo. It was run by a pair of Hungarian immigrants who had recently moved to America, Gabor Csupo and his wife, Arlene Klasky. Klasky Csupo employed three animators.

Groening assumed the animators would clean up his drawings and add details. Instead they just traced over his quickly made black-and-white sketches. Compared to the way the characters would appear in later years, the original sketches look like crude "caveman drawings,"[41] according to Brooks. The task of adding color was handed over to freelance color designer, Gyorgyi Peluce, another

Hungarian immigrant. She decided to give the Simpsons yellow skin and gave Marge her trademark blue hair. Peluce commented on her color choices:

> I love color a lot . . . so I want to do something very different, something that was really going to pop, something that would be a lot of fun. If you look at [Matt's original] drawings they're not cartoony. I think they're in a category of their own because it didn't look like anything that was done before. And that's why I wanted to give them a color that didn't look like *anything* else that was done before.[42]

Groening gave each of his Simpsons *characters a distinctive feature that would clearly show up in a silhouette. With Homer, it is a big beer belly; with Marge, it is her towering beehive hairdo; and with Bart, Lisa, and Maggie it is their spiky locks.*

"That's Bart!"

Groening was immensely satisfied with Peluce's choice of colors. He went to work writing scripts for the bumpers, creating situations and dialog for the characters. Groening laid out his scripts on what are called storyboards, which look like pages in a comic book and consist of a series of drawings that show various scenes and character movements as they unfold in an animated film. The drawings are pinned to a corkboard wall and can be moved, removed, or altered to change the look, pacing, and story of a cartoon.

After the storyboards were finished, they were shown to Klasky Csupo animators Bill Kopp, Wes Archer, and David Silverman, who created the bumpers. When it came time to hire voice actors for the Simpsons, Groening chose Dan Castellaneta for Homer and Julie Kavner for Marge. Both were comedians who regularly appeared in sketches on *The Tracey Ullman Show*.

Castellaneta, who does not sound like Homer in real life, was responsible for inventing the character's most famous utterance, "D'oh!" He also gave voice to Grandpa Simpson and kids' television show host Krusty the Clown. Unlike Castellaneta, Kavner's everyday speaking voice sounded exactly like Marge Simpson's rasp.

Voice actress Nancy Cartwright was originally hired to play Lisa. During her audition with Groening, she asked if she could play Bart, who seemed to her like a much more interesting character. Groening described Bart to Cartwright as devious, underachieving, school hating, and clever. When she gave voice to Bart, Groening laughed and told her, "That's it! That's Bart."[43] Cartwright was the only person to audition for Bart, and Groening hired her on the spot. Lisa's voice went to a twenty-two-year-old struggling actress named Yeardley Smith. Actor Hank Azaria, who was unknown at the time, was cast as Moe the Bartender, who appeared in some of *The Simpsons* shorts.

Unlike most Hollywood television productions, which involve numerous writers, directors, producers, and network executives, *The Simpsons* bumpers were a simple matter. Groening arrived at the studio once a week with a two-page script. He handed it over to the animators, who worked up to sixteen hours a day creating the cartoons.

The Simpsons Movie

Matt Groening first considered making a full-length animated film of *The Simpsons* in 1989. But it was not until 2001 that Groening wrote an initial script for a film. Over the next five years, the script was rewritten more than one hundred times by writers who worked on *The Simpsons* TV show. Animation began on the film in 2006. Groening rejected the idea of using computer-generated imagery, preferring the imperfect look of hand-drawn animation.

The Simpsons Movie premiered in 2007, eighteen years after Groening initially conceived the idea. The plot of *The Simpsons Movie* is based on environmental concerns. Springfield Lake becomes so polluted that US president Arnold Schwarzenegger drops a huge glass dome over Springfield to contain the pollution. The Simpson family escapes through a sinkhole and moves to Alaska. When the Simpsons learn that Schwarzenegger plans to destroy Springfield, the family returns and saves the town.

The Simpsons Movie made more than $527 million worldwide and received high praise from critics and the general public. Groening described his feelings about the film: "Everything in the movie is bigger. In a way, if every episode of 'The Simpsons' is a celebration, which we try to make it, then the movie is like a big celebration. It's a way of honoring the animators, allowing them to really strut their stuff and really go as far as they can with the art of the handwritten gesture."

Quoted in Edward Douglas, "The Creators of *The Simpsons Movie*!," ComingSoon.net, July 24, 2007. www.comingsoon.net.

Once the animation was finished, Groening worked with the voice actors as they recorded their lines.

During this period, Groening was famous for his casual dress; he wore cut-off shorts, sandals, and faded Hawaiian shirts. Brooks affectionately recalled the man behind the first bumpers: "During the early Tracey [Ullman] days, around 1986, Matt was this scruffy presence on the outskirts of our activities, this guy doing independent pieces for the show."[44]

Groening's Dream

The Simpsons bumpers first appeared on *The Tracey Ullman Show* on April 19, 1987. Compared to the sophisticated half-hour show *The Simpsons* would become, the original characters were not well developed. Homer was little more than an angry, negligent dad, and Marge was a typical devoted TV mom. Bart and Lisa fought and played pretend like normal kids. However, a lot of ideas from *Life in Hell* were incorporated into the bumpers.

The Tracey Ullman Show was filmed before a live audience. Ullman often spent hours between sketches changing costumes. To keep the audience entertained during the long breaks, the crew would run all of the *Simpsons* bumpers one after the other. The cartoons received bigger laughs than Ullman. However, each bumper cost $15,000 to produce, and Fox wanted to discontinue the spots. Brooks used his considerable influence to retain network financing of *The Simpsons* and to develop the sketch into a standalone show.

Groening's bumpers appeared on three seasons of *The Tracey Ullman Show*, which struggled to find a loyal audience. Although television critics loved the show, it never caught on with the general public. *The Tracey Ullman Show* was canceled in 1990.

"Around 1986, Matt was this scruffy presence on the outskirts of our activities, this guy doing independent pieces for [*The Tracey Ullman Show*]."[44]

—James L. Brooks, cocreator of *The Simpsons*.

The Ullman show was one of many problems for the new network. Most of Fox's original programming was panned by critics, and many shows only ran for a few months before facing cancellation. Viewers were not tuning in to Fox.

By 1989 Fox executives were desperate. They were not sure *The Simpsons* would be a hit. They reluctantly agreed to produce thirteen half-hour episodes of the animated show, which would run at 8:00 p.m. on Sundays. Fox was taking a risk; no one was sure whether an audience would tune in for a prime-time animated series. However, Brooks felt optimistic about the show's possibilities: "The shorts were getting a great audience response, and Matt had always had this dream of making a prime-time animated program, which was not something that was done at the time."[45]

Alternative to Mainstream Trash

Groening said his goal with the show was to "offer an alternative to the audience, and show them there's something else out there than the mainstream trash that they are presented as the only thing."[46] In order to carry out Groening's wishes, Brooks negotiated a contract with Fox that prevented the network from interfering with the show's content in any way. This was only possible because Fox was struggling; network executives almost always meddle with a show's content. *The Simpsons* was the only show on TV where executives were forbidden from giving notes, or suggestions concerning dialog, plot lines, and characters.

> "[I wanted to] offer an alternative to the audience, and show them there's something else out there than the mainstream trash that they are presented as the only thing."[46]
>
> —Matt Groening, cocreator of *The Simpsons*.

Brooks and Groening added a third cocreator to *The Simpsons*. Sam Simon was an experienced writer who had worked on many successful TV shows. As head writer of *The Simpsons*, Simon assembled a writing staff that included John Swartzwelder, Jon Vitti, Mike Reiss, Al Jean, and others. This team is now legendary in Hollywood. *Simpsons* writer and producer Josh Weinstein described the writers as "comedy gods."[47]

Among the comedy gods in the writers' room, Simon often wrote the funniest lines. As *The Simpsons* cocreator, he defined the looks and personalities of memorable characters originally sketched out by Groening, including Mr. Burns, Dr. Hibbert, Chief Wiggum, and Krusty the Clown.

When *The Simpsons* premiered on December 17, 1989, it was an instant hit. Viewers tuned in by the millions, and TV critics almost universally praised the show. *The Simpsons* satirical look at middle-class America featured the same mixture of wit and despair found in Groening's *Life in Hell* comic strip. Bart, Lisa, Homer, and Marge, even the family dog, faced family hardships while floundering in outrageous social predicaments. The malfunctioning town of Springfield provided a framework for *The Simpsons'* writers to parody nearly every aspect of American culture and society. The show's incisive humor took aim at Springfield authority figures, including the police, teachers, politicians, and bosses. The show skewered corporations, religious zealots, and even the television industry itself.

At school Bart the underachiever and Lisa the overachiever had to deal with cynical teachers, a clueless principal, two-faced friends, and playground bullies. Homer was the family breadwinner, but he was also incompetent, lazy, and temperamental. He gorged on food and spent his free time at Moe's Tavern drinking beer. By placing Homer as a safety administrator at a nuclear power plant, the writers mocked corporate America and its carelessness concerning the environment.

Despite its social commentary, *The Simpsons* never lectured viewers, and the jokes were never mean or nasty. The show's gentle humor was broad; it appealed to a wide spectrum of viewers. For younger viewers there were pratfalls aplenty, slapstick humor in which physical pain was used for laughs. Mature viewers appreciated the show's latest cultural references from films, television, music, and current events. Delivered in rapid-fire succession, the jokes often flew by so quickly that viewers missed some on initial viewings. *The Simpsons* also added numerous catchphrases to the English language, including Homer's "D'oh!," Bart's "Ay caramba!," Nelson Muntz's "*Ha*-ha," and Mr. Burns's drawn-out "Excellent." *Los Angeles Times* critic Joe Morgenstern described the show in its first year:

> "The Simpsons" is a prodigy of pop culture if ever there was one, a prime-time cartoon series that's livelier and more vividly human than most live-action shows. . . . It's a startlingly bold,

often outrageous, depiction of contemporary life as a comic chaos where values are garbled, feelings are ignored and loved ones keep colliding like bumper cars at an amusement park.[48]

Unlike most TV cartoons, which are created for children, *The Simpsons* appealed to kids, trendy teens, and hip adults. By early 1990 the show was attracting nearly as many viewers as its Sunday night competition, the top-rated *Cosby Show*.

Bartmania

During the first season Bart was the lead character in *The Simpsons;* the stories were all about him. By May 1990, when the season ended, Bart was one of the biggest stars in Hollywood. He was featured in cover stories by the leading magazines of the day, including *Time*, *TV Guide*, and *Newsweek*. The attention helped set off a wave of what was called "Bartmania." Bart Simpson merchandise flooded into stores, and the yellow, spiky haired character seemed to be everywhere. His face appeared on T-shirts, mugs, posters, toys, and even air fresheners.

At one point Fox was selling 1 million Bart T-shirts a day. With captions like "Underachiever, and proud of it," "I'm Bart Simpson. Who the hell are you?," and "Don't have a cow, man,"[49] the shirts offended some people. Protesting parents and conservative political groups coerced the department store JCPenney into removing the upsetting T-shirts from a *Simpsons* in-store boutique that featured the show's merchandise. In some schools principles even banned Bart T-shirts. When informed of this development, Groening issued a statement: "I have no comment. My folks taught me to respect elementary school principals, even the ones who have nothing better to do than tell kids what to wear."[50]

> "[The Simpsons is] a startlingly bold, often outrageous, depiction of contemporary life as a comic chaos where values are garbled, feelings are ignored and loved ones keep colliding like bumper cars at an amusement park."[48]
>
> —Joe Morgenstern, *Los Angeles Times* media critic.

Bart Simpson was one of Hollywood's biggest stars by 1990. During the height of "Bartmania" his face appeared on T-shirts, coffee mugs, toys, and even air fresheners.

Clashing Personalities

By 1990 Groening had grown extremely rich in a very short time, but not everyone at the show was happy with his success. Troubles began after Groening became a public figure and the face of *The Simpsons*.

Groening gave dozens of interviews to newspapers and magazines. Many of the early articles lavished praise on Groening for work that was actually done by professional animators and comedy writers. Some who labored over the show felt that Groening was taking credit for all their hard work.

Groening also clashed with Simon, who was known among *The Simpsons* production staff as something of a mad genius. Simon yelled at writers who offered lame jokes, called people obscene names, and rarely compromised when the quality of the show was at stake. His personality was the complete opposite of Groening, who was easygoing and willing to listen to others.

Simon was openly critical of Groening when he tried to contribute to the scripts. He felt Groening did not know how to write clever jokes or invent interesting concepts that could carry a twenty-two-minute animated show.

"The Show's Ambassador"

The conflict between Groening and Simon was aired in an interview the two men gave to the *Washington Post* not long after *The Simpsons* premiered. A defensive Groening told the interviewer, "My contribution to the writing of the show should not be minimized. I'm involved with every creative aspect, from the conception of ideas to writing scripts to directing the voices to designing characters." Simon responded by saying Groening "is doing a lot of other stuff for the show, merchandising and things like that. He's the show's ambassador."[51]

> "[Groening] is doing a lot of other stuff for the show, merchandising and things like that. He's the show's ambassador."[51]
>
> —Sam Simon, *Simpsons* cocreator and head writer.

Despite Groening's assertions, he did not write scripts for *The Simpsons*. However, many news articles implied that Groening wrote all the jokes, drew all the cartoons, and directed all the episodes. The press loved the idea of an American success story; Groening was perceived as a struggling artist whose talents made him an overnight success. However, many of those who worked on *The Simpsons* believed the show's success was largely due to Brooks and Simon, entertainment industry insiders who produced numerous popular sitcoms. *Simpsons* writer Jay Kogen explains:

> If you look at the original *Simpsons* cartoons, those are closer to Matt's drawings, Sam reshaped them and redrew them. He had experience in sitcoms. He had also worked in animation, and was also a very talented cartoonist himself. He's really smart and handled storyboards and all that stuff. He knew what he was doing all the way down the line. And then the story that broke was, "Independent Cartoonist Changes TV."[52]

Simon left *The Simpsons* in 1993 but continued to collect $20 million to $30 million a year for his role in creating the show. He used his wealth to establish the Sam Simon Foundation, which builds shelters for abandoned dogs and trains service dogs for disabled veterans and others. Simon also created the Feeding Families program to provide food for homeless families. Simon gave away most of his fortune before his death from cancer and age fifty-nine in March 2015.

A Host of Imitators

If there is one rule in Hollywood, it is that every successful show will spawn numerous imitators. This was particularly true for *The Simpsons*. By the time Simon quit, prime-time TV hours were filling up with animated comedies.

Animator Mike Judge was among the first to take advantage of the cartoon boom. He created *Beavis and Butt-head*. First broadcast on MTV in 1993, the show followed Beavis and Butt-head, two characters that made Bart Simpson look like a high achiever by comparison. Beavis and Butt-head were lewd, crude, amoral, and ignorant. Their humor was classified as cringe worthy, off color, and shocking.

In 1997 Judge joined forces with *Simpsons* writer Greg Daniels to create *King of the Hill*. The animated series, broadcast after *The Simpsons* on Sunday night, satirized the manners and traits of a fictional family in small-town Arlen, Texas. Another duo who wrote for *The Simpsons*, Al Jean and Mike Reiss, worked with Brooks to create *The Critic*, an animated show about a film snob who reviews movies. The Comedy Central network began airing *South Park* in 1997, another animated satire featuring foul-mouthed boys.

The Best TV Show of All Time

While some of the new animated shows were highly praised, *The Simpsons* remained at the top. By 1999 the show was watched by more than 60 million people weekly in more than sixty countries around the world. During its first decade, *The Simpsons* earned Fox's parent company, Rupert Murdoch's News Corp, around $2 billion and played a major role in the network's growth.

Much of the fortune was generated by merchandise. It was not unusual for the show to receive one hundred requests a day from sellers eager to latch onto the popularity of *The Simpsons*. By 1999 Groening was at the center of a *Simpsons* media and marketing empire. His office was a mess—filled with *Simpsons* lunch boxes, bubble gum, underwear, notebooks, Bart dolls, fan mail, fan scripts, and merchandising offers. Since he owned a major portion of the marketing rights, Groening was obsessed with approving everything featuring the Simpsons. As he recalled in one interview, "I spend a lot of the day being shown things and saying, 'Yes, yes, no, no, yes.'"[53]

In 1999 *The Simpsons* was named the best TV show of all time by *Time* magazine, and the magazine named Bart one of the one hundred most influential people of the twentieth century. By 2000 Groening freely admitted the daily task of writing the show was left to a team of writers whom he called his "Harvard-grad-brainiac-bastard-eggheads."[54] Groening also said he was not even qualified to be an animator on *The Simpsons* due to his limited drawing ability.

Through his fights over creative control of *The Simpsons*, Groening engaged in a tug of war with the show's other creators. Sometimes *The Simpsons* was pulled in three different directions. But as is often the case in Hollywood, alternative thinkers and mad geniuses produce great television. With tension and tempers running high behind the scenes, *The Simpsons* permanently changed television and the way the world sees the typical American family.

CHAPTER FOUR

Into the *Futurama*

In 1999 the forty-five-year-old Matt Groening peered into the future—far into the future. Following his success with *The Simpsons*, Groening set his sights on the thirty-first century. His vision led him to create the animated series *Futurama*. Groening's vision of the year 3000 included interstellar space travel, one-eyed humanoids, extraterrestrial space monsters, and a drunken robot.

Despite numerous technological advances, some things in Groening's thirty-first century had changed very little. Life was still hell, love was still hell, and childhood was still hell. And above all, work was still hell.

Futurama follows the deeds of a well-meaning but hapless pizza delivery boy, Philip J. Fry, whose story begins on New Year's Eve 1999. Fry delivers a pizza to a cryogenics lab, where human bodies are put into a state of suspended animation by freezing. The lab is deserted, and Fry realizes that the delivery order was a prank. Fry dejectedly reviews his sad life while people celebrate in the streets outside. At one minute to midnight, Fry accidentally falls into one of the cryogenics tanks, where he remains until 2999.

Fry awakens in the city of New New York seconds before the New Year. He meets Leela, a shapely one-eyed mutant. Fry immediately falls in love with Leela, who responds with indifference. Groening explains why he created the Leela character with one eye: "The standard depiction of a sexy woman in science fiction is tank top, buxom, two eyes. So I thought, Okay, one eye. Can we make one eyeball sexy? I think we did."[55]

Fry also meets the cigar-chomping robot Bender in the first episode. Bender is another *Futurama* character that breaks science fiction stereotypes. Bender uses alcohol for fuel, but it also makes him drunk, obnoxious, and cruel. The robot swears, steals, and thinks up devious plots that harm other characters. As Groening describes Bender: "He's our robotic Homer Simpson. He's just totally corrupt—lovably corrupt—a la Homer. Loves his vices. I think he's the first robot in science fiction who shoplifts."[56]

Bender, Fry, Leela, and other *Futurama* characters work for an interstellar delivery company called Planet Express. It is run by the aged, absent-minded professor Hubert J. Farnsworth, a distant nephew of Fry's. The company's crew of misfits also includes a Jewish lobster named Dr. John A. Zoidberg and a Jamaican Rastafarian bureaucrat called Hermes Conrad. Like other Groening creations, the characters have bulging eyes, distinctive silhouettes, and overbites. Even the Planet Express spaceship, designed by Groening, featured a pronounced overbite.

In Groening's future many twenty-first-century problems remain, including substance abuse, air pollution, and global warming. However, all the problems are more extreme. Groening described *Futurama*: "It's just like right now, but with a few more death rays, annoying robots, and hideous mutants. So, it's actually pretty much like right now."[57]

> "[The universe of *Futurama* is] just like right now, but with a few more death rays, annoying robots, and hideous mutants. So, it's actually pretty much like right now."[57]
>
> —Matt Groening, cocreator of *The Simpsons*.

Growing Up with Science Fiction

Although *Futurama* began production in 1999, Groening began work on the show in 1994. According to Groening, the idea of *Futurama* "comes from having grown up reading science fiction and—even before I read science fiction, my older brother Mark had a huge collection of science fiction books and magazines. And I loved those covers."[58]

When he was designing *Futurama*, Groening revisited the science fiction novels and comic books of his youth. He also watched numerous science fiction films and TV shows. During this period Groening took extensive notes, filling several hundred pages with

Futurama characters, concepts, and situations. Groening took the name of the show from the popular Futurama pavilion at the 1939 New York World's Fair, which showed a prediction of how life would be twenty years in the future, in 1959. Sponsored by General Motors, the Futurama vision of the future featured an automated highway system where vehicles were controlled electronically and coupled together like train cars. Groening designed the opening sequence of *Futurama* based on this idea.

Matt Groening began work on the animated series Futurama *in 1994. His characters include Leela, the shapely one-eyed captain of the Planet Express; Fry, the twentieth-century pizza delivery boy who was cryogenically frozen (by accident); and Bender, the obnoxious egomaniacal robot.*

Hollywood Bullies

When Matt Groening was producing *Futurama,* he often clashed with network executives who did not like the dark, twisted humor in the show. In a 1999 interview with *Mother Jones* magazine, Groening described his frustrations with Hollywood:

> You can't believe what babies people are. It's really like being in junior high school. [With] the bullies, and every step of the way, any time I've been gracious, that has been—it's seen as a sign of weakness. And every time I've yelled back, I've been treated with respect. That's just not very good psychology. The other thing is, it's just astonishing to have this lesson repeated over and over again: You can't expect people to behave in their own best interest. It's in Fox's best interest for [*Futurama*] to be a success, but they'd rather mess with the show and have them fail, than allow creators independence and let them succeed. . . . There are in Hollywood, film, and TV, whole battalions of junior execs whose job seems to be saying, "Hmmm . . . no."

Quoted in Brian Doherty, "Matt Groening," *Mother Jones*, March/April 1999. www.motherjones.com.

"*The Simpsons* in the Future"

In 1997 Groening partnered with David X. Cohen, a former writer for *Beavis and Butt-head* and *The Simpsons*. Cohen had the perfect résumé to write a science fiction show. Before he worked as a comedy writer, Cohen attended Harvard University and the University of California–Berkeley. He earned degrees in physics (the study of matter, space, energy, and time) and computer science. Cohen was also a major fan of science fiction.

When it came time to sell Fox on his new animated series filled with unconventional characters, Groening attended a three-hour meeting with network executives. As Groening recalls, "The way I sold the show was by saying, 'This is *The Simpsons* in the future,' and dollar signs danced in front of their eyes."[59] Fox had been asking Groening to create another show for years, and network executives were very excited about *Futurama*. After the one meeting, Fox agreed to produce thirteen episodes of the new series, which would be shown after *The Simpsons* on Sunday night.

Despite Groening's description of *Futurama* to Fox, the show was very different from *The Simpsons*. As Groening describes it: "We wanted to do a workplace comedy. 'The Simpsons' was about children and married parents; 'Futurama' is about people in between, they're growing up and haven't settled down. Every other cartoon show seemed to be, you know, dumb dad, bratty kids."[60]

Dr. Farnsworth is perhaps the best representative of the workplace of the future. He is an insensitive boss who willingly risks the lives of his employees, sending them to the ends of the universe to deliver a package. *Futurama* did more than satirize work, as Groening told *Wired* magazine: "The themes: If you are a loser, is it possible to reinvent yourself? How do you deal with the desire for youth, for the return of dead loved ones, and what does it mean to be finite in the universe?"[61]

Futurama appeared at a time when the most popular science fiction films were the *Star Wars* and *Star Trek* series. But Groening, with his alternative viewpoint, did not want to imitate the warlike themes prevalent in those blockbuster films. As Groening stated: "Science fiction for the most part operates on a New Age military motif. If we can just follow orders from our benevolent captain then we can defeat the outside evil and everything will be great. . . . I imagine [with *Futurama*] a corporate, commercial, confusing world where the military is just as stupid as it is currently."[62]

In Groening's vision of the corporate-run future, soft drinks contained mind-numbing narcotics, social media sites are called Facebag and Twitcher, and advertising is beamed into peoples' heads as they sleep. The number one television show in the thirty-first century is *The Mass Hypnosis Hour*. When people watch it, they simply stare blankly at the screen, their minds devoid of thought.

> "Every other cartoon show seemed to be, you know, dumb dad, bratty kids."[60]
>
> —Matt Groening, cocreator of *The Simpsons*.

Futurama also takes on politics, with the heads of dead presidents kept alive in jars. The president of Earth is the head of Richard Milhous Nixon, a caricature of the thirty-seventh president of the United States. During his second term in office, the real-life Nixon was a leading figure in the Watergate break-in scandal, was threatened with impeachment, and resigned in disgrace in 1974. These events occurred during Groening's late teens and helped shape his political outlook. According to Groening: "Ever since I was a kid the Republican politicians have seemed like villainous buffoons. Since Richard Nixon. He was such a cardboard villain. All these guys since seem to be more of the same. I have this obsession with Nixon. On *The Simpsons*, Milhouse is named after him. On *Futurama*, we made Nixon's head in the jar president of Earth."[63]

While Nixon in a jar controls Earth, the universe is run by a villain named Mom who runs MomCorp, a takeoff of the name of Rupert Murdoch's News Corp, which owns Fox. Mom is very wealthy from manufacturing Mom's Old-Fashioned Robot Oil and wears a fat suit in ads to make her appear more lovable to the masses.

Making Matt Crazy

Groening was much more involved in the day-to-day operations of *Futurama*. He worked alongside Cohen and the show's writers and animators to devise jokes, plot lines, and characters. And Groening was pleased to work on *Futurama* without James Brooks and Sam Simon, with whom he often clashed on *The Simpsons*. However, it was Brooks who kept Fox executives from interfering with the content and direction of *The Simpsons*. Groening quickly discovered that without Brooks to block them, Fox executives wanted greater control over *Futurama*. Executives gave Groening numerous notes on ways to change the show to make it more appealing to mainstream audiences. As Groening states, "The second they ordered [*Futurama*], they completely freaked out and were afraid the show was too dark and mean-spirited, and thought they had made a huge mistake and that the only way they could address their anxieties was to try to make me as crazy as possible with their frustrations."[64]

Predictably Groening was not shy about his unhappy relationship with Fox. He said getting *Futurama* on the air was "the worst experi-

Former president Richard Nixon speaks to supporters in 1978 during his first public appearance since resigning from the presidency. In Futurama, *a caricature of Nixon's head appears in a jar and serves as the cartoon's president of Earth.*

ence of my adult life."[65] Groening was outspoken in interviews and often described the network in unflattering terms. As he told *Mother Jones* magazine in 1999, "I guess I shouldn't have been surprised, because this is how everyone is treated [in Hollywood]. But I thought I would have a little bit more leeway since I made Fox so much money with *The Simpsons*."[66]

Even as Groening fought to produce *Futurama*, his personal life was falling apart. Groening had been married to Deborah Caplan Groening since 1986 and had two sons and a daughter. However, the couple divorced in 1999. According to Groening, "The demise of a

Putting the Science in Science Fiction

David X. Cohen earned a degree in physics from Harvard University. When he became the producer and head writer for *Futurama,* Cohen used his scientific knowledge to include jokes in the show about space, matter, light, energy, and time. He also hired writers with similar interests. This resulted in one of the smartest scientific animated sitcoms ever created. Science writer Alaina G. Levine interviews Cohen, who describes the science in *Futurama*:

> With an [ever-present] devotion to physics, and many writing colleagues on the show with backgrounds in applied math, electrical engineering, computer science, and chemistry themselves, Cohen is always looking for places in stories where he can insert "an in-joke" relating to science and technology. He is extremely proud of the fact that Futurama is one of the "few shows that can put in a joke for a physics graduate student.". . .

> Cohen gets such a kick out of imbedding television episodes with scientific citations that after his shows air, he sometimes trolls the internet to read fan comments about his contributions. . . . "One thing I worry about is that when we purposely present inaccurate science in Futurama in the name of entertainment, that viewers may hold it against us," [Cohen] concedes. "We do have genuine respect for science, and we're trying, when we can, to raise the level of discussion of science on television. If we fail sometimes, I hope people still appreciate the frequent attempts to bring real science into the show."

Alaina G. Levine, "The Futurama of Physics with David X. Cohen," APS Physics, 2010. www.aps.org.

family is unbelievably painful, to a degree I hadn't anticipated, and the amount of lingering grief can't be quantified. I thought everything was on a track and was going to stay that way for a long time, and I didn't expect to be living alone."[67]

Unhappy Fox

Futurama's run at Fox was also painful; the network seemed unable to properly promote the off-beat comedy. When the show premiered at 8:30 p.m. on Sunday, March 28, 1999, it earned the highest-rated debut in Fox history and was watched by 25 percent more viewers than *The Simpsons*. However, after the premiere, Fox moved *Futurama* to Tuesday night. In this era before the advent of digital video recorders, some fans were not aware of the shift or did not follow the transition to its new time. And even as the new time slot confused viewers, Fox remained unhappy about the tone of show. According to Groening, "The network really—really was freaked out by the show, the suicide booths—and lobster creatures and Bender being so anti-social."[68]

The suicide booths that troubled Fox were called Stop-and-Drop. They resembled twentieth-century phone booths. For a quarter, users could pick deaths ranging from quick and painless to a clumsy bludgeoning. In one *Futurama* episode, Fry enters the booth to make a phone call but manages to escape before it kills him. Groening got the idea for the suicide booths from a 1937 Donald Duck cartoon, *Modern Inventions*, in which Donald visits the Museum of Modern Marvels. Donald tries to use several coin-operated devices, which nearly kill him.

Fox did not get the joke about suicide booths, which were used in several episodes. Yet despite its misgivings, Fox picked up *Futurama* for a second season in 2000. At that time the show was moved back to Sundays at 8:30 p.m. However, halfway through the season *Futurama* was moved again, to Sundays at 7:00 p.m., the show's third position in less than a year.

Awards and Cancellation

Despite the lack of support from Fox, *Futurama* had a loyal audience and was critically acclaimed. The show won a Primetime Emmy Award for Outstanding Animated Program every year it was on the air. It also won numerous Annie Awards, which are presented for animation.

Futurama was especially popular among people interested in science and professional scientists of all types. Episodes accurately depicted scientific theories about black holes in space, time travel, and the big bang that created the universe. Cohen relied on his background in physics to insert sly jokes into the show that might only be understood by those with advanced scientific knowledge.

One of Cohen's favorite tricks was to make jokes in what he called alien languages. The jokes were really written with Latin letters and symbols created by animators. Each alien language letter or symbol had a corresponding letter in the English language. Thousands of sharp-eyed viewers hit their pause buttons to freeze the screen and working out ways to decipher the jokes. These were shared on *Futurama* websites, where many fans excelled in alien language translation.

Although scientists and critics may have loved *Futurama*, Fox felt the show was not attracting enough viewers to justify the expensive animation production process. However, the show's problems were partially the fault of the network. During *Futurama*'s fourth season, in 2003, the show was often preempted for Sunday night sporting events or news specials. With its unpredictable schedule, viewer numbers fell. Fox decided to stop producing new episodes of *Futurama* while never formally canceling the show. Midway through the 2003 season, *Futurama* went off the air. Reruns of *Futurama*'s seventy-two episodes were shown on the Cartoon Network from 2003 to 2007.

Direct to DVD

The cancellation of *Futurama* surprised Groening, who had several more scripts ready for production. As Groening stated, "In my heart of hearts, I thought the show was too good to end like that."[69] However, *Futurama* took on a new life after it went off the air. Fox released DVDs in four volumes with all the original episodes from each season. The DVDs showed impressive sales figures, prompting Fox to continue production of *Futurama*. The network made a deal with Groening to produce four new, movie-length (ninety-minute) episodes. They would be sold as direct-to-DVD productions, not shown on network TV.

Groening described the themes of the films: "We [planned] these four movies—one was time travel, next was sword-and-sorcery, third was a space monster movie and the last one is a grand ecological science fiction epic which also has some emotional payoffs for the characters if you've been following the series from the beginning."[70] The emotional payoff Groening referred to concerns Fry and Leela finally admitting their love for one another and kissing.

The first *Futurama* film, *Bender's Big Score*, was released in November 2007. The film was a continuation of the series, with smart comedy, insane science fiction predicaments, and an elaborate time-travel sequence. There were special guest appearances by the rapper Coolio, former vice president Al Gore, and comedian Sarah Silverman.

Bender's Big Score, *the first* Futurama *movie, was released in 2007. It continued the exploits of the TV series characters and included special guest appearances by rapper Coolio, former vice president Al Gore, and comedian Sarah Silverman.*

The other *Futurama* films were released in 2008 and 2009. Although they were originally produced only to be sold or rented on DVD, Groening made a deal with Comedy Central. The movies were divided up into sixteen half-hour episodes that aired on the comedy network.

When the first segment of *Bender's Big Score* premiered on Comedy Central on June 24, 2010, it was the most-watched prime-time show in the network's history. Comedy Central decided to continue producing *Futurama*, and Groening and Cohen created twenty-six more half-hour episodes for the network.

Smart and Sophisticated

Around the time the last *Futurama* film was released, *The Simpsons* was once again making headlines. The show celebrated its twentieth anniversary in January 2009. At that time, *The Simpsons* had become the longest-running prime-time show in television history. It was shown in ninety countries throughout the world.

The Simpsons was even watched at the Vatican, the home of the pope and the administrative center of the Roman Catholic Church. The Vatican newspaper *L'Osservatore Romano* congratulated Groening and praised *The Simpsons'* realistic and smart writing. Surprisingly, the Vatican appreciated how *The Simpsons* portrayed Reverend Lovejoy's sermons as boring and self-serving. Homer's face-to-face discussions with God about the uncertainty of life were also singled out. Groening offered his own thoughts on the popularity of his animated creations:

> "The Simpsons" basically—and "Futurama"—are really smart shows. They're kind of disguised as these goofy animated sitcoms, but the references within the shows, if you're paying attention, are pretty smart and pretty sophisticated. And if you don't get it, it's OK—you have a nice entertainment experience—but if you've gone to college and seen a few movies, you can appreciate the shows on a much more satisfying level.[71]

Back in Springfield

Although *Futurama* may have been smart, the show suffered from steadily declining ratings on Comedy Central. In 2010 an average 2.6

million viewers tuned in. That number fell to 2.3 million in 2010 and bottomed out at 1.7 million in 2012, when the show was canceled.

Throughout its run, *Futurama* was nominated for seventeen Annie Awards, winning seven, and twelve Emmy Awards, winning six. *Futurama* was also nominated four times for a Writers Guild of America Award and won twice.

While *Futurama* was beginning its seventh and final season in 2012, Groening celebrated another milestone: *The Simpsons* aired its 500th episode in February. At that time Groening answered a question that had been on the minds of fans for years; in which state was Springfield located? In an interview with *Smithsonian* magazine, Groening revealed that the Simpsons' hometown was Springfield, Oregon. Groening said that he never wanted to tell, because "Springfield was one of the most common names for a city in the U.S. In anticipation of the success of the show, I thought, 'This will be cool; everyone will think it's their Springfield.' And they do."[72]

In honor of the 500th *Simpsons*, Groening engaged in some philanthropy. He donated $500,000 to the School of Theater, Film and Television (TFT) at the University of California–Los Angeles. The money created the Matt Groening Chair in Animation, which will fund visiting artists. Groening donated another $100,000 to the school to support students making animated shorts with socially responsible themes. Teri Schwartz, dean of the TFT, praised Groening for his gifts to the school: "Matt Groening is recognized globally as a preeminent and pioneering animator, storyteller, cartoonist, writer and producer. His groundbreaking animated series have truly changed the landscape of television and have become a gold standard for animation and great storytelling throughout the entertainment industry."[73]

> "[Matt Groening's] groundbreaking animated series have truly changed the landscape of television and have become a gold standard for animation and great storytelling throughout the entertainment industry."[73]
>
> —Teri Schwartz, dean of the School of Theater, Film and Television at the University of California–Los Angeles.

D'oh!

Matt Groening celebrated his sixtieth birthday in 2014 while *The Simpsons* aired its twenty-fifth season. At that time, his show starring world-class underachievers was achieving unprecedented global greatness. During every half hour of every day, *The Simpsons* was being broadcast somewhere in the world. Over 150 million people watched the show every week. And Homer's catchphrase "D'oh!" was even added to the Oxford English Dictionary.

In interviews Groening stated that he wished he could produce *Futurama* episodes into the foreseeable future. With a net worth of around $550 million, Groening probably could afford to produce the show by himself. But whatever Groening's future holds, *Life in Hell*, *The Simpsons*, and *Futurama* have already made their mark on history.

From his grade-school drawings of Rotten Rabbit to his high school novel featuring Bart Simpson, Groening mined his creative impulses to maintain his sanity in a crazy world. Through luck, determination, and rewarding partnerships with others, Groening used his early influences to create a cast of characters people could relate to no matter where in the world they lived.

Although Groening might not be as famous as Bart, Homer, or Lisa, his characters have long given voice to his fears, quirks, and concerns. And Groening's creations have allowed him to take on the authorities he resented as a kid and reduce them to cartoon parodies.

While mocking authorities, Groening's influential shows often feature positive messages. However bad the situation in each episode, there is always a happy ending; the characters do the right thing for the greater good. While reflecting both the good and the bad of American culture, Groening provides his viewers with problems, solutions, and dozens of laughs per minute.

SOURCE NOTES

Introduction: For the Love of "Everyman"

1. Quoted in Simpson Crazy, "Matt Groening," 2012. www.simpsoncrazy.com.

2. Matt Groening, *The Simpsons Handbook*. New York: Harper-Collins, 2007, p. 3.

3. Quoted in Carina Chocano, "Matt Groening," *Salon*, January 30, 2001. www.salon.com.

Chapter One: Growing Up Groening

4. Quoted in Stacey Wilson, "'The Simpsons' at 500: Untold Stories," *Hollywood Reporter*, February 8, 2012. www.hollywoodreporter.com.

5. Quoted in Barbara Beck, "Cartoon Family from Hell: Matt Groening's 'The Simpsons' Are Moving to a Prime-Time Spot on Fox," *Philly.com*, January 12, 1990. http://articles.philly.com.

6. Quoted in Joe Morgenstern, "Bart Simpson's Real Father," *Los Angeles Times*, April 29, 1990. http://articles.latimes.com.

7. Quoted in Paul Andrews, "The Groening of America," *Seattle Times*, August 19, 1990. http://community.seattletimes.nwsource.com.

8. Quoted in Steve Heisler, "Here's Every Single Thing Bart Simpson Ever Wrote on the Chalkboard from the Opening Credits of *The Simpsons*," A.V. Club, February 16, 2012. www.avclub.com.

9. Quoted in David Shulman, "Matt Groening: Life Is Swell," *LA Weekly*, July 18, 2007. www.laweekly.com.

10. Quoted in Claudia De La Roca, "Matt Groening Reveals the Location of the Real Springfield," *Smithsonian*, May 2012. www.smithsonianmag.com.

11. Quoted in Simpson Crazy, "Matt Groening."

12. Quoted in Kristine McKenna, "Matt Groening," *The Simpsons Archive*, April 14, 2001. www.snpp.com.

13. Quoted in Mark Rahner, "Matt Groening to Give Grads Bart-like Wisdom?," *Seattle Times*, June 9, 2000. http://community .seattletimes.nwsource.com.

14. Quoted in Andrews, "The Groening of America."

15. Quoted in Andrews, "The Groening of America."

16. Quoted in Andrews, "The Groening of America."

17. Quoted in Morgenstern, "Bart Simpson's Real Father."

18. Quoted in Morgenstern, "Bart Simpson's Real Father."

19. Quoted in Morgenstern, "Bart Simpson's Real Father."

20. Quoted in Christopher Borrelli, "Groening, Barry Still Draw upon Each Other," *Chicago Tribune*, November 7, 2009. http:// articles.chicagotribune.com.

Chapter Two: Life in Hell

21. Quoted in Richard von Busack, "'Life' Before Homer," Metroactive, November 2, 2000. www.metroactive.com.

22. Quoted in Morgenstern, "Bart Simpson's Real Father."

23. Quoted in David Sheff, "Matt Groening," David Sheff.com, June 2007. http://davidsheff.com.

24. Quoted in Von Busack, "'Life' Before Homer."

25. Quoted in John Ortved, *The Simpsons: An Uncensored, Unauthorized History*. New York: Faber and Faber, 2009, p. 19.

26. Quoted in Ortved, *The Simpsons*, p. 17.

27. Quoted in Morgenstern, "Bart Simpson's Real Father."

28. Glen Weldon, "Binky, We Hardly Knew Ye: Groening Ends His *Life in Hell* Comic Strip," NPR, June 20, 2012. www.npr.org.

29. Quoted in Alex Pappademas, "R.I.P., *Life in Hell*," *Grantland* (blog), June 21, 2012. http://grantland.com.

30. Quoted in Simpson Crazy, "Matt Groening."

31. Quoted in Robert Lloyd, "Life in the 31st Century," *LA Weekly*, March 24, 1999. www.laweekly.com.

32. Quoted in Joanne Kaufman and Cindy Yorks, "*Life in Hell*'s Matt Groening Goes Overboard to Make the Simpsons the First Family of TV 'Toons," *People*, December 18, 1989. www.people.com.

33. Quoted in Ortved, *The Simpsons*, p. 23.

34. Quoted in Ortved, *The Simpsons*, p. 24.

35. Quoted in Colin Marshall, "Before *The Simpsons*, Matt Groening Illustrated a 'Student's Guide' for Apple Computers (1989)," Open Culture, April 10, 2014. www.openculture.com.

36. Quoted in Alan Paul, "Matt Groening," *The Simpsons* Archive, November 7, 1999. www.snpp.com.

37. Matt Groening, *The Big Book of Hell*. New York: Pantheon, 1990, p. v.

38. Ted Rall, "Matt Groening Ends *Life in Hell*," *Ted Rall* (blog), June 20, 2012. http://rall.com.

Chapter Three: The Simpsons Conquer the World

39. Quoted in Simpson Crazy, "Matt Groening."

40. Quoted in Ortved, *The Simpsons*, p. 28.

41. Quoted in Jackson Burke, "James L. Brooks," *The Simpsons* Archive, September 22, 2002. www.snpp.com.

42. Quoted in Ortved, *The Simpsons*, p. 52.

43. Quoted in Nancy Cartwright, *My Life as a 10-Year-Old Boy*. New York: Hyperion, 2000, p. 41.

44. Quoted in Morgenstern, "Bart Simpson's Real Father."

45. Quoted in Burke, "James L. Brooks."

46. Quoted in Ken Tucker, "'Toon Terrific," *The Simpsons* Archive, May 7, 1998. www.snpp.com.

47. Quoted in Ortved, *The Simpsons*, p. 58.

48. Morgenstern, "Bart Simpson's Real Father."

49. Quoted in *People*, "Eat My Shirts! Pesky Bart Simpson Tees Off a California Principal—and Gets Kicked Out of School for Swearing," May 21, 1990. www.people.com.

50. Quoted in Scott Williams, "Bratty Bart's Attitude Too Radical for Some Dudes," *Spokesman (WA)-Review*, May 23, 1990, p. A2.

51. Quoted in Ortved, *The Simpsons*, p. 58.

52. Quoted in Ortved, *The Simpsons*, p. 64.

53. Quoted in McKenna, "Matt Groening."

54. Quoted in Chocano, "Matt Groening."

Chapter Four: Into the *Futurama*

55. Quoted in Sheff, "Matt Groening."

56. Quoted in Joe Earley, "An Interview with Matt Groening," Got *Futurama*, February 22, 1999. www.gotfuturama.com.

57. Quoted in Brian Doherty, "Matt Groening," *Mother Jones*, March/April 1999. www.motherjones.com.

58. Quoted in Peter Roth, "An Interview with Matt Groening," Got *Futurama*, 2010. www.gotfuturama.com.

59. Quoted in James Sterngold, "Bringing an Alien and a Robot to Life: The Gestation of the Simpsons' Heirs," *New York Times*, July 22, 1999. www.nytimes.com.

60. Quoted in Robert Lloyd, "Matt Groening's 'Futurama' Is Ready for Its Intergalactic Send-Off," *Los Angeles Times*, July 5, 2013. http://articles.latimes.com.

61. Quoted in Kevin Kelly, "One-Eyed Aliens! Suicide Booths! Mom's Old-Fashioned Robot Oil!," *Wired*, February 1999. http://archive.wired.com.

62. Quoted in Kelly, "One-Eyed Aliens! Suicide Booths! Mom's Old-Fashioned Robot Oil!"

63. Quoted in Sheff, "Matt Groening."

64. Quoted in Doherty, "Matt Groening."

65. Quoted in Chocano, "Matt Groening."

66. Quoted in Doherty, "Matt Groening."

67. Quoted in McKenna, "Matt Groening."

68. Matt Groening, "Commentary: I, Roommate," Infosphere, December 21, 2008. http://theinfosphere.org.

69. Quoted in Joe Rhodes, "Back to the Animated Future, This Time on DVD," *New York Times*, November 27, 2007. www.nytimes.com.

70. Quoted in Todd Leopold, "Matt Groening Looks to the Future," CNN, February 26, 2009. www.cnn.com.

71. Quoted in Leopold, "Matt Groening Looks to the Future."

72. Quoted in Kimberly A.C. Wilson, "Matt Groening Says the Springfield of 'The Simpsons' Is Named for Springfield, Oregon," *Oregonian* (Portland, OR), April 10, 2012. www.oregonlive.com.

73. Quoted in Kathleen Miles, "Matt Groening Gets a Hollywood Star on Eve of *The Simpsons'* 500th Episode," *Huffington Post*, February 14, 2012. www.huffingtonpost.com.

IMPORTANT EVENTS IN THE LIFE OF MATT GROENING

1954
Matthew Abram "Matt" Groening is born in Portland, Oregon, on February 15.

1961
The eight-year-old Groening wins a short-story contest held by *Jack and Jill* magazine, an entertainment and education publication for young readers.

1964
Homer Groening makes a short film based on a story his son Matt made up about a brother and sister having an adventure.

1969
Groening writes part of an unfinished novel featuring a character named Bart Simpson.

1973
Groening graduates from Lincoln High School in Portland, Oregon.

1977
Groening graduates from Evergreen State College in Olympia, Washington, and moves to Hollywood.

1978
Groening's *Life in Hell* comic strip is published for the first time, in the culture and arts magazine *Wet*.

1980
Life in Hell begins a decades-long run in the *Los Angeles Reader*.

1984
Groening publishes *Love Is Hell*, his first book consisting of previously published *Life in Hell* strips.

1985
Groening and Deborah Caplan found Life in Hell Inc. to sell *Life in Hell* merchandise.

1987
The first animated *Simpsons* shorts appear on *The Tracey Ullman Show*.

1989
The Simpsons premiers as a thirty-minute, prime-time animated sitcom on the Fox Network.

1990
The popularity of *The Simpsons* results in a summer of Bartmania, a run on T-shirts and other merchandise featuring Bart Simpson.

1999
Futurama premiers on Fox and achieves the highest rating of any debut in the network's history.

2003
Fox cancels *Futurama*.

2007
The first direct-to-DVD *Futurama* film, *Bender's Big Score*, is released. *The Simpsons Movie* premieres in theaters.

2010
New *Futurama* episodes run on Comedy Central.

2012
After creating 1,669 *Life in Hell* comics, Groening stops drawing the strip.

2014
The Simpsons begins it twenty-fifth season, with 150 million people tuning in every week worldwide.

FOR FURTHER RESEARCH

Books

Hillary L. Chute, *Outside the Box: Interviews with Contemporary Cartoonists*. Chicago: University of Chicago, 2014.

Noell K. Wolfgram Evans, *Animators of Film and Television: Nineteen Artists, Writers, Producers and Others*. Jefferson, NC: McFarland, 2011.

Kathy Furgang, *Careers in Digital Animation*. New York: Rosen, 2013.

Matt Groening, *The Book of Hell*. New York: Pantheon, 1990.

Matt Groening, *The Simpsons Handbook*. New York: Harper Design, 2007.

Matt Groening, *The Simpsons/Futurama Crossover Crisis*. New York: Abrams, 2010.

Stuart A. Kallen, *Animation*. San Diego: ReferencePoint, 2015.

Jeff Lenburg, *Matt Groening: From Spitballs to Springfield*. New York: Chelsea House, 2011.

Websites

Futurama (www.cc.com/shows/Futurama). The official Comedy Central website for *Futurama*, with video clips, character biographies, scheduled showings, merchandise, and links to social media sites.

Got *Futurama* (www.gotfuturama.com). A comprehensive *Futurama* fan site, with character biographies, episode guides, multimedia 3-D artwork from fans, videos, original drawings, games, screensavers, wallpapers, and alien codecs.

Infosphere (http://theinfosphere.org). The Infosphere is the *Futurama* Wiki site, with more than thirty-four hundred articles that anyone can edit. The site contains information about episodes, descriptions of every character, written transcripts of comments by Matt Groening and others taken from DVDs, and community discussions.

No Homers Club (www.nohomers.net). The No Homers Club is a *Simpsons* discussion site founded in 2001 by fans of the show. The site features forums, images, information, and news.

Simpson Crazy (www.simpsoncrazy.com). One of the most thorough fan sites on the web, Simpson Crazy features *Simpsons* news, episode guides, scripts, music and song lyrics, print comics, character biographies, interviews with voice actors, and much more.

The Simpsons **Archive** (www.snpp.com). The Internet repository operated by fans concerning everything *Simpsons*. The archive holds articles, interviews, writers and directors' lists, essays on dozens of characters, foreign language files, and even discussions of smoking, religion, and food on the show.

Films

Bender's Big Score, DVD. Directed by Dwayne Carey-Hill. Los Angeles, CA: Curiosity Company, 2008. A beautifully animated film that follows the antics of *Futurama* characters, including Bender the Robot, who is possessed with a malicious virus.

The Simpsons Movie, DVD. Directed by David Silverman. Los Angeles, CA: Gracie Films, 2007. A full-length feature film produced by Matt Groening about America's favorite, bright yellow family from Springfield. Created with hand-drawn animation rather than computer generated imagery, the film involves a polluted lake, a giant pig, and a dome descending on Springfield.

INDEX

Note: Boldface page numbers indicate illustrations.

PICTURE CREDITS

Cover: © Paul Mounce/Corbis

AP Images: 31

© Armando Aroriza/Zuma Press/Corbis: 49

© Ken Hawkins/Zuma Press/Corbis: 16

© Wally McNamee/Corbis: 59

© Christopher J. Morris/Corbis: 24

Photofest Images: 12, 28, 39, 42, 55, 63

© Fred Prouser/Reuters/Corbis: 8

Maureen Vana/Zuma Press/Newscom: 20